Heroes for Young Readers

Written by Renee Taft Meloche
Illustrated by Bryan Pollard

Adoniram Judson
Amy Carmichael
Betty Greene
Cameron Townsend
Corrie ten Boom
David Livingstone
Eric Liddell
George Müller

Gladys Aylward
Hudson Taylor
Jim Elliot
Jonathan Goforth
Lottie Moon
Mary Slessor
Nate Saint
William Carey

Heroes of History for Young Readers

Written by Renee Taft Meloche
Illustrated by Bryan Pollard

Clara Barton
George Washington
George Washington Carver
Meriwether Lewis

…and more coming soon

*Heroes for Young Readers Activity Guides and audio CDs
are now available! See the back of this book for more information.*

For a free catalog of books and materials contact
YWAM Publishing, P.O. Box 55787, Seattle, WA 98155
1-800-922-2143, www.ywampublishing.com

HEROES OF HISTORY FOR YOUNG READERS

MERIWETHER LEWIS

Journey Across America

Written by Renee Taft Meloche
Illustrated by Bryan Pollard

Emerald
Books
P.O. BOX 635
LYNNWOOD, WA 98046

Meriwether Lewis: Journey Across America   Text © 2006 by Renee Taft Meloche   Illustrations © 2006 by Bryan Pollard
Published by Emerald Books, P.O. Box 635, Lynnwood, WA 98046   ISBN 1-932096-27-2   Printed in China.   All rights reserved.

A boy named Meriwether Lewis
    thought the greatest thrill
was hunting and exploring Georgia's
    forests and its hills.

He crept through brush in search of insects
    and of plants that grew.
He saw opossums, beavers, and
    sometimes a bear or two.

In seventeen eighty-three, when he
    was only nine years old,
this young lad spotted Indians
    nearby his own household.

He and his family left their cabin
    on a moonless night
and hid out in the forest, hoping
    they'd not have to fight.

They made a fire and threw on
      some corn gruel they could eat.
A war cry sounded. Meriwether
      jumped up on his feet
and threw a pot of water on
      the flames immediately.
The Indians left; they were confused
      because they could not see.

Though others there had panicked when
      they felt under attack,
young Meriwether's mind was calm,
      which helped him to react.

He'd later learn that people are
      the same, whatever color,
for some have better qualities
      and characters than others.

He moved back to Virginia, where
    he'd lived when very young,
for now a big plantation there
    was left for him to run
because his dad had passed away.
    And yet it soon was clear
he longed to be back in the woods
    with marigolds and deer.

When old enough he joined the army,
    met a captain there—
a tall man, slender, with a ready
    smile and red hair.

His name was William Clark, and as
    the two became good friends,
they never dreamed what great adventures
    lay in store for them.

The army needed someone who'd
be faithful and sincere
to help deliver soldiers' pay
across the wild frontier.

When Meriwether got the job,
he galloped over land
with money in his saddlebags,
reins firmly in his hand.

Years later Thomas Jefferson—
    the U.S. president—
asked Meriwether to explore
    his country's continent.

He'd have him take a team of men
    out west so they could scout
a way to the Pacific Ocean
    just by river routes.

Soon Meriwether said he'd go.
    Before his team embarked,
he asked that his co-leader be
    his good friend William Clark.

They left by boat in summertime
    in eighteen hundred three.
They carried food and things to trade
    with Indians they'd see.

They took the Mississippi River
    and Missouri too.
They fought strong currents and debris,
    determined to get through.

Collecting things from nature,
   Meriwether spent his days
detailing all he saw, which left
      him breathless and amazed.

He saw two curious animals
   he'd never seen before:
a badger and coyote. There
      was so much to explore.

A year went by. He and his team
emerged upon new ground—
the Great Plains with their open spaces
and new sights and sounds.

They met with the Missouri and
the Oto Indians,
and William gave them U.S. flags.
They started to be friends.

They saw large herds of buffalo,
    so very grand in scope.
They got their first look at some prairie
    dogs and antelope.

They also met the Sioux tribe, which
    was always on the go.
This tribe pulled up their teepees and
    they followed buffalo.

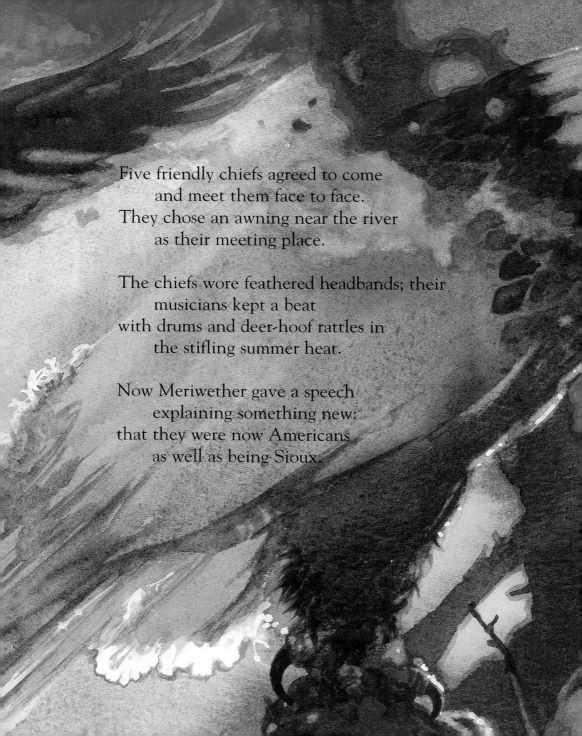

Five friendly chiefs agreed to come
    and meet them face to face.
They chose an awning near the river
    as their meeting place.

The chiefs wore feathered headbands; their
    musicians kept a beat
with drums and deer-hoof rattles in
    the stifling summer heat.

Now Meriwether gave a speech
    explaining something new:
that they were now Americans
    as well as being Sioux.

He said, "Our white man's government
    now owns all native land,
and we are family underneath
    the Great White Chief's command.
Please try to live in peace with all
    the red men and the white.
We all must try to get along
    and fairly trade, not fight.
We'll set up trading posts for you
    to show you many things,
like rifles, knives, and iron tools
    for your considering."

The chiefs agreed and Meriwether
    felt quite satisfied.
He did not know they wanted weapons
    to fight other tribes,
but tribes upon the plains had warred
    for many generations.
It would take time for them to change
    this hostile situation.

Clark passed out medals showing natives
    shaking hands with whites.
The flip side showed the president.
    Then long into the night,
young boys showed off their skill by shooting
    arrows into trees
while warriors danced around a fire.
    Everyone seemed pleased.

Then William Clark and Meriwether
    traveled with their men
into a Mandan village and
    were treated just like friends.

The Mandan asked the team to join
    them on a buffalo hunt.
The Mandan men rode hard and fast
    and always stayed in front.

They galloped at hair-raising speeds
    across the grassy plains,
their knees dug in their horses' sides,
    their bows and arrows aimed.

They swiftly killed some buffalo,
    then skinned and cooked the meat.
They shared it with the white men, who
    ate well for many weeks.

Months passed, then Meriwether went
    by foot and took four men
in search of waterfalls, and as
    he stepped around a bend,
he heard a rumble farther on.
    The sound began to grow.
Cascading falls splashed downward in
    a never-ending flow.

These "Great Falls" had five waterfalls
    that stretched twelve miles long.
He thought, *We'll have to lug canoes*
    and manage to go on
to reach the very top—and worse—
    the only route to take
is filled with wolves, ferocious bears,
    and deadly rattlesnakes.

And so they carried their canoes
    up over rocks and thorns
that ripped right through their moccasins
    until their feet were torn.

They kept on ferrying one by one—
    while bleeding, sore, and bruised—
their loaded-down canoes until
    the last one had been moved.

They traveled onward, higher, climbing
    up above the falls.
No longer could they see wide plains
    or buffalo at all.

They struggled on upriver in
    the sweltering summer heat,
and as they went caught glimpses of
    fleet-footed mountain sheep.

They'd soon need horses for the Rocky
    Mountains they would climb
and knew that the Shoshone tribe
    had steed they hoped to find.

So Meriwether, with three men,
    set out to look one day.
They hiked and hiked until they spotted—
    not too far away—
a native woman with two girls.
    As Meriwether neared,
the woman shook with fear. He gave
    her beads and then a mirror.

Soon she was smiling with her girls.
    The gifts had been approved.
Then Meriwether heard the thunder
    of strong horses' hooves.

Shoshone warriors raced up and
    the woman showed her beads—
a present from the white men, which
    put all much more at ease.

Their chief jumped right down from his mount,
    convinced they'd come in peace.
He greeted Meriwether warmly,
    pressing cheek to cheek.

Then Meriwether traded musket
    balls and several knives
for thirty horses; an old man
    agreed to be their guide.

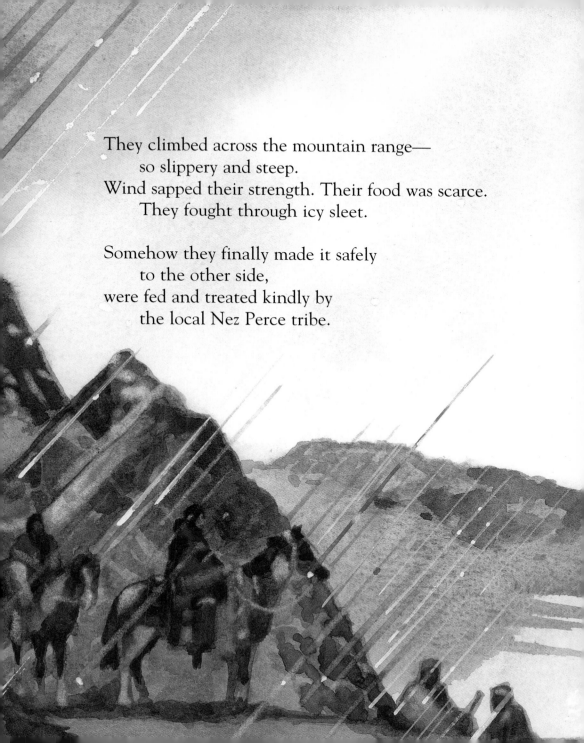

They climbed across the mountain range—
    so slippery and steep.
Wind sapped their strength. Their food was scarce.
    They fought through icy sleet.

Somehow they finally made it safely
    to the other side,
were fed and treated kindly by
    the local Nez Perce tribe.

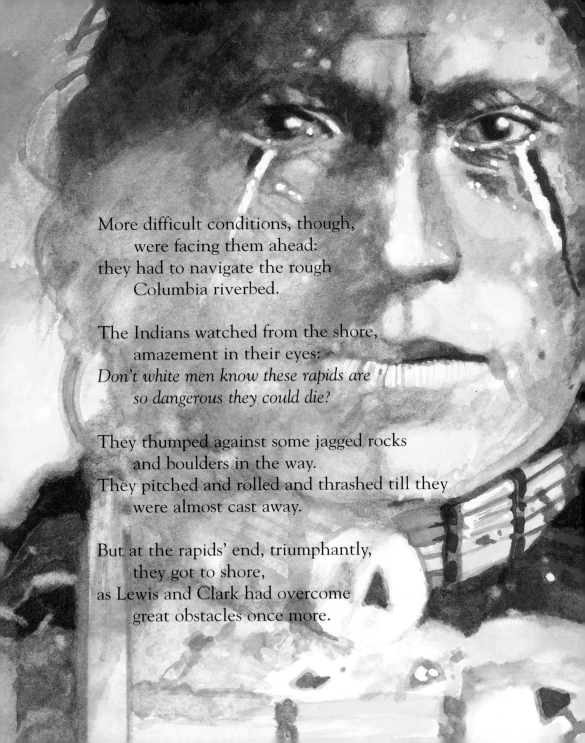

More difficult conditions, though,
        were facing them ahead:
they had to navigate the rough
        Columbia riverbed.

The Indians watched from the shore,
        amazement in their eyes:
Don't white men know these rapids are
        so dangerous they could die?

They thumped against some jagged rocks
        and boulders in the way.
They pitched and rolled and thrashed till they
        were almost cast away.

But at the rapids' end, triumphantly,
        they got to shore,
as Lewis and Clark had overcome
        great obstacles once more.

A few weeks later, smells of salt
    hung strongly in the air.
One man let out a holler of
    delight: "Look over there!"

The great Pacific Ocean!
    They cheered in celebration.
They'd come more than four thousand miles
    to reach their destination.

They spotted whales and smooth blue dolphins
    swimming just offshore.
They marveled at this ocean's coastline
    they could now explore.

They built a fort for winter as
    it rained until it poured;
then in the spring they started back
    the way they'd come before.

Returning home took just six months
    instead of many years.
The people of St. Louis rushed
    to meet them with loud cheers.

Soon Meriwether saw the president,
    and he explained
about the animals he'd seen,
    the Indians, plants, and plains.

He showed maps he and William drew
    of newly scouted ground,
and though a water route clear to
    the ocean was not found,
it really did not matter for
    what happened in the end
is that he found a way by land *and*
    water with his friend.

He had the courage to explore
vast unknown land out west.
As an explorer he, with Clark,
had been our country's best.

Christian Heroes: Then & Now

by Janet and Geoff Benge

Adoniram Judson: Bound for Burma
Amy Carmichael: Rescuer of Precious Gems
Betty Greene: Wings to Serve
Brother Andrew: God's Secret Agent
Cameron Townsend: Good News in Every Language
Clarence Jones: Mr. Radio
Corrie ten Boom: Keeper of the Angels' Den
Count Zinzendorf: Firstfruit
C.T. Studd: No Retreat
David Livingstone: Africa's Trailblazer
Eric Liddell: Something Greater Than Gold
Florence Young: Mission Accomplished
George Müller: The Guardian of Bristol's Orphans
Gladys Aylward: The Adventure of a Lifetime
Hudson Taylor: Deep in the Heart of China
Ida Scudder: Healing Bodies, Touching Hearts
Jim Elliot: One Great Purpose
John Williams: Messenger of Peace
Jonathan Goforth: An Open Door in China
Lillian Trasher: The Greatest Wonder in Egypt
Loren Cunningham: Into All the World
Lottie Moon: Giving Her All for China
Mary Slessor: Forward into Calabar
Nate Saint: On a Wing and a Prayer
Rachel Saint: A Star in the Jungle
Rowland Bingham: Into Africa's Interior
Sundar Singh: Footprints Over the Mountains
Wilfred Grenfell: Fisher of Men
William Booth: Soup, Soap, and Salvation
William Carey: Obliged to Go

Heroes for Young Readers and Heroes of History for Young Readers are based on the Christian Heroes: Then & Now and Heroes of History biographies by Janet and Geoff Benge. Don't miss out on these exciting, true adventures for ages ten and up!

Continued on the next page...

Heroes of History

by Janet and Geoff Benge

Abraham Lincoln: A New Birth of Freedom
Benjamin Franklin: Live Wire
Christopher Columbus: Across the Ocean Sea
Clara Barton: Courage under Fire
Daniel Boone: Frontiersman
Douglas MacArthur: What Greater Honor
George Washington Carver: From Slave to Scientist
George Washington: True Patriot
Harriet Tubman: Freedombound
John Adams: Independence Forever
John Smith: A Foothold in the New World
Laura Ingalls Wilder: A Storybook Life
Meriwether Lewis: Off the Edge of the Map
Orville Wright: The Flyer
Theodore Roosevelt: An American Original
William Penn: Liberty and Justice for All

...and more coming soon. Unit study curriculum guides are also available.

Heroes for Young Readers Activity Guides
Educational and Character-Building Lessons for Children

by Renee Taft Meloche

Heroes for Young Readers Activity Guide for Books 1–4
Gladys Aylward, Eric Liddell, Nate Saint, George Müller

Heroes for Young Readers Activity Guide for Books 5–8
Amy Carmichael, Corrie ten Boom, Mary Slessor, William Carey

Heroes for Young Readers Activity Guide for Books 9–12
Betty Greene, David Livingstone, Adoniram Judson, Hudson Taylor

Heroes for Young Readers Activity Guide for Books 13–16
Jim Elliot, Cameron Townsend, Jonathan Goforth, Lottie Moon

...and more coming soon.

Designed to accompany the vibrant Heroes for Young Readers books, these fun-filled activity guides lead young children through a variety of character-building and educational activities. Pick and choose from the activities or follow the included thirteen-week syllabus. An audio CD with book readings, songs, and fun activity tracks is available for each Activity Guide.

For a free catalog of books and materials contact
YWAM Publishing, P.O. Box 55787, Seattle, WA 98155
1-800-922-2143, www.ywampublishing.com